WORKS ON PAPER

Also by Jennifer Barber:

Vendaval
Rigging the Wind
Given Away

Works on Paper

POEMS

Jennifer Barber

WINNER OF THE 2015 TENTH GATE PRIZE

THE WORD WORKS
WASHINGTON, D.C.

The Word Works
P.O. Box 42164
Washington, D.C. 20015
editor@wordworksbooks.org

Cover art: Beth Balliro
Cover design: Susan Pearce
Author photograph: Zoë Brown

LCCN: 2015958916
ISBN: 978-0-944585-02-0

Acknowledgments

Thanks to the editors of the following journals, in which the poems below first appeared:

Bellevue Literary Review: "Despondency"
Cerise Press: "Benign"
Ibbetson Street: "Last Photograph"
Jewish Forward: "Gomorrah" and "Rainbow Lake"
masspoetry.org: "Before October"
Mishkan haNefesh: Machzor for the Days of Awe: "Past the Gates of the City" (as "The Gathering")
Missouri Review: "Motion Harmony #1," "Motion Harmony #2," "Motion Harmony #4," "Commuter Rail" (as "Station"), "Nests," and "Inscription"
Osiris: "In August" (in altered form)
Pangyrus: "Motion Harmony #3" (in altered form)
Poetry: "Before Dark" and "I Found a 1950s 'Answer and Color-in Book'"
Poetry Kanto: "L.B.," "The Dozen White Irises," "Trope," "After a Year," and "Five Starts"
Post Road: "Cabin" and "Judenplatz"
Solstice: "Assembling a Psalm" and "September: One of the Psalms"
Upstreet: "7 A.M.," "Rooms," "Galway, Fireplace," and "Reading Taha Muhammad Ali"

"Last Photograph" was also featured on *Poetry Daily*. "From 'Hebrew Prayers Made Easy'" appeared in *Kisufim: Identity and Otherness*, eds. Hava Pinchas-Cohen, Gershon Giron, The Euro-Mediterranean Institute for Inter-Civilization Dialogue.

I wish to thank Peter Brown, Cherie Collins, Linda Cutting, and Carol Dine for their early reading of many of these poems. I'm grateful to the first readers of the manuscript, Jessica Greenbaum, Ellen Kaufman, Fred Marchant, David Ferry, and George Kalogeris.

Leslie McGrath and Nancy White of The Word Works have been insightful and supportive editors; I appreciate their generosity, dedication, and artistry.

Contents

for Pete, Jeff, and Zoë

and in memory of Louis and Jane Barber

Part 1

Source

The sound of rain arriving before it arrives
has no sound to speak of, but it does

say something to the leaves, something the leaves
know how to take; they're leaning toward

the place where the rain is about to begin,
drawing nearer together but widening

the surface of their urgency, their need
to register each shifting of the air.

The sky darkens; the leaves have darkened too.
The waiting is hard to bear, resembling

other kinds of waiting, waiting to hear
in a waiting room, in the afternoon,

in the moments that seem to move apart
before they become whatever's to come.

Inscription

It must have been you
in the back of my mind

all along—I imagine you
picking up an apple

without taking a bite,
my poems open on your lap,

the easy way you concentrate
but just as easily drift.

The effect I wanted
might not come across:

where I put a caesura, or when
a line breaks into another

is not as luminous—
in spite of my obsessiveness—

as I hoped it might be.
I can't explain the difference

between longing and fear,
how to tell them apart,

when to give over to pleasure.

Motion Harmony #1

By nightfall
    the first rain
        reaps a summer's worth of leaves.

How did
    Sappho arrange her hair?
        When and for whom did she let it down?

The moon
    naked as a slate
        impossible to write on or ignore.

Tell me
    what we are
        tonight and can you make it true?

Country Aubade

For a rooster's mud-red crest.
For the shuffle of an ox.

With the drooping eyes
of an owl at first light.

In the damp of the day,
in a bed that shifts like straw.

Our weighted hips—
our tapering thighs.

Something has happened here;
something is happening.

Rooms

I held my son, my daughter,
I set them down.

*

I washed my daughter's hair,
both of us in the bath,

I watched her hair
rise, a fan around
the full moon of her head.

*

My son, stringing
superhero figures to our plants,
chair legs, table legs.

He put them in a box,
forgetting the one he hung
from the radiator's ridge.

*

A boy called my daughter
to accuse her of cruelty
(she wasn't in love with him).

She ran to his house
in a downpour,
waited for him.

Later, he rang our bell,
rain dripping from his hair.

*

My son, home for a visit,
met his friends at midnight—
he came home at five—
we passed each other in the hall.

*

Their rooms resemble their rooms,

the floor looks at the ceiling, which looks at the floor,

the window open to the wind.

*

My daughter took the blue notebook
of the hours she kept to herself.

My son left behind
a sweater, a pair of jeans,
a crumpled page of sheet music.

She took a swollen suitcase.
He left a keychain that lights in the dark.

Almanac

In Virgil's poem
on when to plow, to plant,

how to tend to
livestock and vine,

there is a passage about
a herd of shaggy cattle

in a northern land.
They stand around

in the bitter cold,
shifting on their hooves.

Bits of snow and ice
cling to the coarse

auburn hair of their coats.
They gaze out from

behind their forelocks,
seeing the frozen ground

with patient eyes.
The poet also tells

which moon to plant beneath
once the soil has turned

a shade of red,
and which grape,

ripened a dark gold,
makes the new wine.

There is a part
about caring for bees,

when to build them a home
woven with bark,

tucked away, out of the wind,
next to a brook

and flowering mint.
All in the hive have a task:

some nurture infants,
the hope of their nation.

Others maintain the comb,
repairing and gluing the cracks.

Those who labor outside
go back and forth

to the blossoming meadow,
carrying pollen

from the purple clover
on the backs of their legs.

They settle in at dusk.
According to Virgil, a king

lives at the very center
of their world.

Who first discovered
it was a queen?

Trope

Morning emerges
like a long egg from a hen.

A gazelle is wearing
antelope pants.

The clouds are baby goats.
The clouds have hooves.

I take my glasses off
the better to see you with

and the leaves
in front of the sun.

Commuter Rail

No one else here.

A few gray feathers drift,
some coarse, some soft,
a few tufts
cling to the curb

and then more
touch my shoes,
so many, it's impossible
not to step back,
to look up—

a falcon on
the overhang,
absorbed, methodical,
taking a pigeon apart.

Which weighs more,
a pound of feathers
or a pound of lead?

She holds the body
in its place
with her talon,
plying the hook of her beak.

The Etching "Four Bulls in Midair"

One is upside down,

belly exposed, horns parentheses,
tail outstretched, as in a storm

the wind had flung him from his field.

Another drifts sideways,
eye shrunken in fear.

The third is floating with legs wide.

It's as if the grass that fled
were gone forever, like the thought

of something making sense again.

The fourth has an old man's gaze.
Even Goya doesn't know he knows

what to make of what he sees.

Benign

The thought of more waiting rooms
and the need for bravery recede.

Small things matter again:
a cardinal in the winter pine,

the wristwatch misplaced.
At night I get into bed with *The Death*

of Ivan Ilych and read of his last three days,
his struggle with the black sack

he imagines surrounding him—
I put the book aside. The wind

roughs up the highest branches of the oak.
The ear opens like an eye.

—Unable to fit in the sack
or work free of it, he howls and howls.

The Dozen White Irises

The one bud that tried to bloom
stopped halfway, a yellow stripe

where the anther left a trace.
The others pucker like fingertips.

They whisper among themselves,
This is all we get, our throats

won't grow translucent in the light,
the white flame we might have raised

is only an inward wintering.

Nests

In the knifelike cold of March,
the nests are waiting it out,

bleak as abandoned forts:
they don't know whether

any beaked and flying thing
will return to their sticks

and rotted leaves,
the droppings, the dried glue.

Abraded by ropes of wind,
unable to come apart,

the disheveled walls
keep nothing in but the dark:

it's as if they never were
an ear to the fledgling

cries that touched the clouds,
charged with birth and hunger.

Five Starts

Post-op

My appendix, gone; my table of contents remains

Site

The nest that cleaves to a high branch,
                    an eye socket in the pine

Trial by Flight

          As if someone poured a pitcher full of moths
at the porch light

Grief

We know how ill he is—
                    no way to stop it—

Question

          Is *bereft* some kind of command?

Last Photograph

The look on his face
isn't acceptance; isn't fear;
neither a need to be among
his children, gathered,
nor a desire to be alone.

It's more like disbelief
through which
the sharp intelligence
is like light through glass,
unable to come to a stop.

Motion Harmony #2

The pears dropped
          by the failing tree
     are pale bronze,
          sunlit with copper spots.
Rotting in the grass.
          Riddled with wasps.

By pear I mean pear,
          not a riddled heart.
     At least I think I do.
          The flesh of it laid bare
by the intricate, steady
          work of mouths.

Cabin

The cheap old *Portable Chekhov*
falls from my hand
with the words "It was evening"
which I know are followed by
"an evening in spring"
and "the regiment in town."

I've turned the metal key
that turns off the lamp,
this room just big enough
for a bed and a night table.

The kiss the awkward, shy
soldier will steal
from a woman in the dark
drawing room will have to wait.
The pine boards of these walls
are a forest of their own.

Before Dark

They used to mass
in the crowns of oaks
on every street for blocks around
but have gone elsewhere,
the evening no longer
gathered by their feathers
but by the leaves, which blot
whatever light is left to the sky.

Whether we saw the crows
as a barely-worth-mentioning
image of death for the way
they took over branches
with perfect authority,
whether, where did I hear it, their
numbers were thinned by disease,
nothing avails. They are

missing, the crackle of wings
against the weight of their flight,
beaks that break open
broadcasting any scrap of news.
Like our children, they carry off
whole years, like the windborne thought
of cries never welcome enough
in our hearing day or night.

Anniversary Window

Whose lilac, whose raspberry bush?

How long have I been a geranium?

This morning, when I woke,
I wore the bedsheet's creases on my cheek.

Which of us will die first? (I think it's you,
but it might be me.)

You look at me, you look away,
you look again, and I look back.

The little white flags on the neighbor's lawn
show the poison has been applied.

A mourning dove blinks in the crab apple.

I've started something but I don't know what.

Motion Harmony #3

The male seahorse
                carries the pearls

         of the female's eggs
                       inside his pouch

where they hatch
              in miniature.

        He does a forward bend,
                  a backward bend.

He's relieved,
             she's stunned.

        Soundless, the little
                fleet sails forth.

After

The breathing oaks.

These days and these nights.

I'm lying in the grass,

holding the broken shoulder of a breeze.

You're beside me in the dark.

My finger loses itself

in the open wound of you.

Three Months

July—The New Plant

Because its leaves
attend to the sound
of water from a pitcher,
startle as soon as the water pours,

it seems their growth
might be clocked
in minutes and seconds,
one leaf, next, and next,

as if the whole plant
were turning in place,
pouring the ripeness of the light
through the valley of its veins.

August—Waves

Some of them are towering
as in a dream,
impossible to swim.

Others rush
each other's arms,

confusing the desire
to embrace
with the desire to dissolve.

September—One of the Psalms

Night is as light as day to you.

You see me where I am. You know
how far back the waking of me goes.

Last night, green stars above the road.

I lit a candle and the flame
was fingernail and lily, tongue;

the blue blade of the flame

cut the night from its stem,
the light from dark, the dark from the dark.

5 A.M.

The first snowfall
of the year

is the first snow
of the year before,

the same blue-purple
dawn, the street, the roofs,

the streetlight's bulb
turning the flakes

visible, like dust
from a drifting soul

radiating silence
as it goes,

neither female nor male;
the soul doesn't

know itself
and then, returning, does.

Near Eastern Creation Myths

Darkness flooding
the face of the deep,
God beginning to form heaven and earth,
a wind sweeping the water—

*

Before the legions of stars
fastened the sky in place,

before land divided
waters above from waters below,

before the earth grew a pelt
—marshes, meadows, reeds—

the first begetters, Great Deep and Mother of All,
gave birth to gods—

*

When no shrubs had yet appeared,
no bush, no tree, no rain,
but groundwater welled up,

the Lord God took a handful of clay
and made a man.
The Lord God breathed
a life breath into the man.

The Lord God planted
a garden in the east.

Four rivers issue from the river there,
one through the land
of abundant gold;
one through the land of Cush;

the third, the Tigris, flowing east of Asshur;
the Euphrates is fourth.

*

After the great battle,
when the leader of the gods
split with his arrow
the Mother of All,
he stretched half of her out as heaven;
he fattened the rest of her as land.

*

The valley, the shadow, the vale,
one slope in sunlight, the other in storm.

Spiny trees of the desert plain.

Spongy tussocks of matted grass,
glowing swollen under the clouds.

*

Who scatters the east wind?
Who pours the mountain streams?

Who cradles the hatchlings?
Who the fissures of the cliff?

Part 2

I Found a 1950s "Answer and Color-in Book"

One day the children played

>in the kitchen.
>in the cellar.
>in the yard.

The yard looked like

>a meadow.
>a forest.
>an island in the sea.

The children forgot their

>mud cakes,
>swing set,
>sticks,

when a girl taught them

>cat's cradle.
>clay people.
>folded paper boats.

Late afternoon, whispering, they lay

in a sandbox.
on the sidewalk.
in the grass.

Each knew the others had

a mother.
a father.
brothers and sisters.

They traded blood oaths that foretold

how close,
how long,
at what cost.

Galway, Fireplace

The way the peat burns
with a low, slow flame
could break your heart
if you wanted
the sound of wood crackling.

You're still cold.
You put on a new briquette
carefully, so as
not to bury the flame,
small and blue as a child's thumb.

Judenplatz

The ochre cornices,
a gallery at one end, a café at the other,
a statue of a playwright
in his morning coat.

Early, the café
empty, the gallery empty,
the owner, red-haired, her keys in hand,
framed by the doorway.

Early, no one's visiting
the concrete memorial
set like a box
in the middle of the Judenplatz.

How are the same
apartment buildings where they were?
How is it that Vienna is
Vienna, waking in this light?

7 A.M.

So cold the wrens puff up
on the juniper,

snowdrifts instead of the drought

real enough in my fleeing
the fires around the trees.

I thought I heard you; I wasn't sure

and besides, the crackling
of the pine needles

would have drowned you out.

At the bottom of the hill,
the cows, set loose

to find what water they could.

Through the surface
of a savannah-reservoir

gray, elephantine rocks

were spreading aprons of sand,
islands and peninsulas.

Wave and shadow overlapped—

hard to tell
the end of day, the end of night.

I waded toward a motorboat,

the buoyant green flickering
algae on me like lace.

I carried a flashlight.

L.B.

September

Only sparrows in the oak
and a hooded crow, exotic to me,

a two-toned back, gray over black.

The undersides of leaves
like mirrors.

"A couple of weeks or months,"
his doctor predicted in July.

"Sometimes we're wrong."

October

A week ago, Outside
was with him still,

around the building and back,
one of us or more.

Today, in the window,
in the trees,

soundless collisions
of light and dark

impossible to divide,
the addictive, flickering

play of the shadows
over the ground.

Variants

He calls the Oxycodone
Oxymoron;

Ativan is Atta Boy.

How does it go, the verse about
the sun not striking us

by day, nor the moon by night?

On Morphine, His Last Words

I have to be there by noon

Here is my forehead,
here is my jaw

Thanks for the visitation, kids

Are these my eyes
under my hand?

Before October

September comes
with its gleaming promises,
the red green silver gold
leaves of the copper beech,
my hand on the smooth trunk.

Standing under those branches,
who could stop
from burnishing the lines
that arrive like birds
making the most of what remains?

The crown of the tree is its own
language, which likes to ask
questions about death.
The leaves toss; their syllables
combine and separate again.

From My Window

Children on their way to school
dawdle, then race each other.

They cross with the police lady.
Inside the school, they have

circle time and snack time, xylophone.
Believing he's got it down,

a child of mine is singing
"Hot Cross Bones" in a big voice.

The teacher puts the instruments away.
The morning, already gone.

My fingers lift a china cup
in the light the blind lets through.

Assembling a Psalm

Where the sun
the cedars
a shadow on the slope

Where our flesh
like grass
and the grass like our flesh

When fever
dissolves my bones
when I don't know where I am

When the turn
there is always a turn
a way to open the lips

To see to stand
to speak to praise
deliver our mouth that wonder fruit

Reading

The man behind me in the library
at the table

near the door
came in after I did; he entered

talking to himself, with barely audible
moans between the words,

and little sighs,
Alright...so...I know...I know it is...

OK...oh...I left the news right there....
Turning, I can't read his face—

is he drunk?
Out of his mind?

I turn back to my book.
The low vibrations of his voice

hush to almost nothing,
then to nothing. Did he leave?

I miss it, his crooner pillow talk
in broad daylight, here.

Gomorrah

Having heard
rumors and cries,
they're at the edge of the city.

What will they
see, what world.

The older messenger steps
through a door
in the wall

that circles
this doomed place
Abraham pleaded to save.

After a Year

Is it an extravagance, this grief?

Is it clean, is it purely itself?

Would I feel it less if he'd been

ready after the treatments

or if he hadn't written in the black-and-white

speckled notebook I bought him,

'Nothing else to try... *how, when?*'

What if he had dreamed

death as light on a windowsill,

shorebirds running at a wave?

The valet

waited across the room,
not a man but a wooden stand.

My sister and I
stroked the back of my father's hand.
He moved his jaw as if answering.

The hospice nurse
said he was growing wings
and would leave us when the wings grew in.

The valet held
a shirt and a sweater and corduroys
from the day before

with its limited
knowledge of the body of a man.

Before Noon

Near the end of the school year,

the children are trying, and failing, to listen,
or failing to try, a warm day that exhales

the leaves that seem to listen to themselves,

the street bracing for the sounds
of the playground, the running steps, the cries

that dissipate on a slow wind

and mingle with the birds calling back and forth,
asking, demanding, to be listened to.

To the River

for D.F.

He packs his bags
for the journey

but leaves them
at home,

bringing only
a hip flask

past the pale
outcropping rock,

the thorns
of the barberry,

down the slope
to the river's edge.

Mud wells
around his shoes.

The woman sitting
on the bank

opposite, in
panels of fog,

stringing beads
in her lap,

doesn't resemble
his wife

but she does.
What stops him

from saying, *Anne?*

Past the Gates of the City

The cattle, the wind,
between the mountains and the sea,
the tent, the faces.

They called you by various names,
none of them yours,
all of them yours.

You knew the hunger of open beaks
high in the cedar.
You watched the infant goats
sway to their feet.

I called you by various names,
all of them yours,
none of them yours.

There was the bread I ate,
the heart of the bread,
the bread of the heart.

God, in the Index

absence of
ambivalence of
anger of
arm of

crying out
like a woman in labor

descending
dwelling in mist

Ehyeh
El Shaddai

as father
as fire cloud

as leopard
as lion
as lord of hosts

as savior
as shepherd
as shield

as voice

as water
as wheat
as wind

Despondency

Mild, persistent, low-grade,
the fever doesn't spike;

it couches in me but never
asks my life or rushes

through with wild adrenaline
to hood me so I wouldn't see

my daughter's face.
Instead it quietly steals

the savor from a day, ignores
the beauty of the lemons

in their net bag, summer light
across a floor; it suspects

the worst of friends,
tamps me down to monotone

for weeks, for months,
then turns to ask

why I've been holding back.
It believes in familiarity,

not-planning, not-imagining
the shapes that follow

from the precincts of the new,
the brightness of the air.

Now and then, it goes
without warning.

Song

The night full of oranges
and the scent of jasmine
blooming on the wall,

the dusty air of boulevards.
Love is what it isn't,
isn't it, and don't we stop

in the place we think we are
only to find it deserted,
swept clear of the breeze

that drew us when we thought
we were the architects
of a season, of that time

in a city far away?
Nothing left of it now
but this warm night.

Before Evening

Flowing in sunlight, the June breeze
poured a flock of shadows through a branch

in shimmering pieces and kept
moving itself among the leaves,

a way to move while staying in place
over the houses and the streets;

it kept flowing toward the first
of July, the day of his scan

that would show if the rounds
of chemo had done their job;

a gorgeous summer, everybody said,
or did they, the coolness of the breeze,

the changing of its shape
passing among the crowns of the trees.

In August

The dusty wideness of the streets
like the contagion's aftermath.

Where are we when we're here?

Let's walk, let's bend the light
above our evaporated steps.

Reading Taha Muhammad Ali

I wondered about the translation
       and how a qasida works,
              whether a gray dove

always nests in its lines,
              a dove and a gray olive tree
       and longing for the girl

the poet loved when he was young.
       Grieving, his qasida sent
              tendrils around and around

his fingers, a pomegranate,
              the well that was a well
       in Saffuriyya, in childhood.

Reading, I couldn't tell
       if saying *qasida* would still
              the traffic on the street below,

if my tendency to mourn
              would let me eavesdrop
       on the red mourning dove

settled in a patch of sun
       on my neighbor's roof,
              if the plea I thought I heard

was a plea, or something
              else, that knows to alight
       and leave all at once.

From "Hebrew Prayers Made Easy"

Exercise 1

that place, that time, those days
a name, the name, his name
a king, to a king, to the king
from the earth, on the earth, from the king

Exercise 2

at this season, on this night
you did not hear, you heard
for the world, of the heavens
this is a blessing, this is a word

Exercise 3

every day, with all your heart
upon your heart, upon your hand
I said to them, you said to us
when you lie down, when you wake

Exercise 4

you said, you remembered, you kept
a heart, in the heart, in my heart
my house, my name, to me, in me
your house, your name, to you, in you

Motion Harmony #4

Harvest is past—

what the moon says to herself
       at the start of another autumn night.

Nothing will be saved.

The moon a doorknob to a dark
       so large no one can see it.

Rainbow Lake

You walked on ahead.
I wanted to go back.
One other car in the lot;

a man got in and drove it away.
A bank of mist
slid past the mountain.

Thunder against
the Divide,
thunder and blue lightning.

The ancient Hebrew
God leapt to mind,
intimate, everywhere.

And Elijah on the slope
after the fire,
after the shattering.

Notes

"The Etching 'Four Bulls in Midair'": the name commonly given to this Goya etching is "Disparate de toritos."

The "Motion Harmony" poems take their titles from musical compositions by Jeffrey Arlo Brown.

"Near Eastern Creation Myths": I turned to the *Jewish Study Bible* (Jewish Publication Society) and W. G. Lambert's *Babylonian Creation Myths* (Eisenbrauns) while working on this poem.

"Three Months": section 3 references Psalm 139.

"Judenplatz": a square in Vienna that was a center of Jewish life in the city.

"L.B.": "the sun not striking us // by day, nor the moon by night" refers to Psalm 121.

"From 'Hebrew Prayers Made Easy'": the phrases in this poem are taken from the textbook *Prayerbook Hebrew the Easy Way*, eds. Joseph Anderson, Linda Motzkin, Jonathan Rubenstein, and Laurence Wiseman (EKS Publishing).

About the Author

Jennifer Barber's collections of poetry are *Given Away* (Kore Press, 2012), *Rigging the Wind* (2003, recipient of Kore's 2002 First Book Award), and *Vendaval*, in *Take Three: 3* (Graywolf Press, 1998).

Her poems have appeared in *Agni*, the *Georgia Review*, the *Gettysburg Review*, the *Missouri Review*, the *New Yorker*, *Orion*, *Post Road*, *Poetry*, *Poetry Kanto*, *Upstreet*, and elsewhere. She teaches literature and creative writing at Suffolk University in Boston, where she is a scholar in residence. She is founding and current editor of the literary journal *Salamander*, published at Suffolk.

About the Artist

Beth Balliro's work in painting and mixed-media has been exhibited nationally, most recently in Ink & Stick, Grand Gallery Louisiana (2015) and Love's Labors, Trustman Gallery of Simmons College, Boston (2012). Her work addresses maternity, family legacy and generational white flight. She teaches at the Massachusetts College of Art & Design, where her research and practice emphasize the development of artists of color in urban communities.

About The Word Works

The Word Works, a nonprofit literary organization, publishes contemporary poetry and presents public programs. Other imprints include the Washington Prize, International Editions, and the Hilary Tham Capital Collection. A reading period is also held in May.

Monthly, The Word Works offers free literary programs in the Chevy Chase, MD, Café Muse series, and each summer, it holds free poetry programs in Washington, D.C.'s Rock Creek Park. Annually in June, two high school students debut in the Joaquin Miller Poetry Series as winners of the Jacklyn Potter Young Poets Competition. Since 1974, Word Works programs have included: "In the Shadow of the Capitol," a symposium and archival project on the African American intellectual community in segregated Washington, D.C.; the Gunston Arts Center Poetry Series; the Poet Editor panel discussions at The Writer's Center; and Master Class workshops.

As a 501(c)3 organization, The Word Works has received awards from the National Endowment for the Arts, the National Endowment for the Humanities, the D.C. Commission on the Arts & Humanities, the Witter Bynner Foundation, Poets & Writers, The Writer's Center, Bell Atlantic, the David G. Taft Foundation, and others, including many generous private patrons.

The Word Works has established an archive of artistic and administrative materials in the Washington Writing Archive housed in the George Washington University Gelman Library. It is a member of the Council of Literary Magazines and Presses and its books are distributed by Small Press Distribution.

wordworksbooks.org

The Tenth Gate Prize

Founded by Series Editor Leslie McGrath, the prize honors the work and poetics of Jane Hirshfield and promotes the work of mid-career poets. American and Canadian poets with two or more published collections may submit between June 1 and July 15. The 2014 winner of the prize was Lisa Sewell for *Impossible Object*. The winner receives publication and a cash prize.

Other Word Works Books

Karren L. Alenier, *Wandering on the Outside*
Karren L. Alenier, ed., *Whose Woods These Are*
Karren L. Alenier & Miles David Moore, eds.,
    Winners: A Retrospective of the Washington Prize
Christopher Bursk, ed., *Cool Fire*
Grace Cavalieri, *Creature Comforts*
Barbara Goldberg, *Berta Broadfoot and Pepin the Short*
Frannie Lindsay, *If Mercy*
Marilyn McCabe, *Glass Factory*
Ayaz Pirani, *Happy You Are Here*
W.T. Pfefferle, *My Coolest Shirt*
Jacklyn Potter, Dwaine Rieves, Gary Stein, eds.,
    Cabin Fever: Poets at Joaquin Miller's Cabin
Robert Sargent, *Aspects of a Southern Story*
    & *A Woman from Memphis*
Nancy White, ed., *Word for Word*

Mel Belin, *Flesh That Was Chrysalis*
Carrie Bennett, *The Land Is a Painted Thing*
Doris Brody, *Judging the Distance*
Sarah Browning, *Whiskey in the Garden of Eden*
Grace Cavalieri, *Pinecrest Rest Haven*
Cheryl Clarke, *By My Precise Haircut*
Christopher Conlon, *Gilbert and Garbo in Love*
    & *Mary Falls: Requiem for Mrs. Surratt*
Donna Denizé, *Broken like Job*
W. Perry Epes, *Nothing Happened*
Bernadette Geyer, *The Scabbard of Her Throat*
Barbara G. S. Hagerty, *Twinzilla*
James Hopkins, *Eight Pale Women*
Brandon Johnson, *Love's Skin*
Marilyn McCabe, *Perpetual Motion*
Judith McCombs, *The Habit of Fire*
James McEwen, *Snake Country*
Miles David Moore, *The Bears of Paris*
    & *Rollercoaster*
Kathi Morrison-Taylor, *By the Nest*
Tera Vale Ragan, *Reading the Ground*
Michael Shaffner, *The Good Opinion of Squirrels*
Maria Terrone, *The Bodies We Were Loaned*
Hilary Tham, *Bad Names for Women*
    & *Counting*
Barbara Ungar, *Charlotte Brontë, You Ruined My Life*
    & *Immortal Medusa*
Jonathan Vaile, *Blue Cowboy*
Rosemary Winslow, *Green Bodies*
Michele Wolf, *Immersion*
Joe Zealberg, *Covalence*

THE WASHINGTON PRIZE

Nathalie F. Anderson, *Following Fred Astaire*, 1998
Michael Atkinson, *One Hundred Children Waiting for a Train*, 2001
Molly Bashaw, *The Whole Field Still Moving Inside It*, 2013
Carrie Bennett, *biography of water*, 2004
Peter Blair, *Last Heat*, 1999
John Bradley, *Love-in-Idleness: The Poetry of Roberto Zingarello*, 1995, 2ND edition 2014
Christopher Bursk, *The Way Water Rubs Stone*, 1988
Richard Carr, *Ace*, 2008
Jamison Crabtree, *Rel[AM]ent*, 2014
Barbara Duffey, *Simple Machines*, 2015
B. K. Fischer, *St. Rage's Vault*, 2012
Linda Lee Harper, *Toward Desire*, 1995
Ann Rae Jonas, *A Diamond Is Hard But Not Tough*, 1997
Frannie Lindsay, *Mayweed*, 2009
Richard Lyons, *Fleur Carnivore*, 2005
Elaine Magarrell, *Blameless Lives*, 1991
Fred Marchant, *Tipping Point*, 1993, 2ND edition 2013
Ron Mohring, *Survivable World*, 2003
Barbara Moore, *Farewell to the Body*, 1990
Brad Richard, *Motion Studies*, 2010
Jay Rogoff, *The Cutoff*, 1994
Prartho Sereno, *Call from Paris*, 2007, 2ND edition 2013
Enid Shomer, *Stalking the Florida Panther*, 1987
John Surowiecki, *The Hat City After Men Stopped Wearing Hats*, 2006
Miles Waggener, *Phoenix Suites*, 2002
Charlotte Warren, *Gandhi's Lap*, 2000
Mike White, *How to Make a Bird with Two Hands*, 2011
Nancy White, *Sun, Moon, Salt*, 1992, 2ND edition 2010
George Young, *Spinoza's Mouse*, 1996

Kajal Ahmad (Alana Marie Levinson-LaBrosse and
Barbara Goldberg, trans., with Mewan Nahro
Said Sofi and Darya Abdul-Karim Ali Najin),
Handful of Salt
Keyne Cheshire (trans.), *Murder at Jagged Rock:
A Tragedy by Sophocles*
Yoko Danno & James C. Hopkins, *The Blue Door*
Moshe Dor, Barbara Goldberg, Giora Leshem, eds.,
The Stones Remember: Native Israeli Poets
Moshe Dor (Barbara Goldberg, trans.), *Scorched by the Sun*
Lee Sang (Myong-Hee Kim, trans.), *Crow's Eye View:
The Infamy of Lee Sang, Korean Poet*
Vladimir Levchev (Henry Taylor, trans.), *Black Book of
the Endangered Species*

CPSIA information can be obtained
at www.ICGtesting.com
Printed in the USA
FSHW011157180621
82505FS

9 781944 585020